CogAT ® - 3rd and 4th Grade Quantitative Battery Practice Questions (Form 7, Level 9 and 10)

Prepare Your 3rd and 4th Grader For The Cognitive Abilities Test - CogAT

By: Sam Khobragade

1) Number Analogies / Quantitative Relationships

120 Analogy Practice Questions

Grade:	3rd and 4th Grade
Level:	Level 9 and 10
Form:	7
Battery:	Quantitative Battery
Section:	1) Number Analogies / Quantitative Relationships

By: Sam Khobragade

1) Number Analogies / Quantitative Relationships : 120 Questions

Analogy 1

[1 → 10]   [534 → 5340]   [474 → ?]

A 4748   B 4268   C 4739   D 4740   E 4264

Analogy 2

[36 → 37]   [24 → 26]   [126 → ?]

P 138   Q 5   R 2   S 134   T 129

Analogy 3

[6 → 18]   [10 → 30]   [12 → ?]

A 24   B 39   C 23   D 40   E 36

Analogy 4

[18 → 37]   [4 → 9]   [14 → ?]

P 16   Q 39   R 17   S 29   T 34

Analogy 5

[1 → 2]   **[18 → 36]**   **[6 → ?]**

A 20   **B** 22   **C** 5   **D** 7   **E** 12

Analogy 6

[162 → 159]   **[72 → 68]**   **[138 → ?]**

P 3   **Q** 135   **R** 6   **S** 133   **T** 141

Analogy 7

[4 → 12]   **[8 → 24]**   **[10 → ?]**

A 21   **B** 38   **C** 19   **D** 30   **E** 29

Analogy 8

[6 → 14]   **[8 → 18]**   **[14 → ?]**

P 40   **Q** 30   **R** 14   **S** 17   **T** 36

Analogy 9

[18 → 37]   [6 → 13]   [14 → ?]

A 15   B 32   C 28   D 29   E 16

Analogy 10

[8 → 19]   [10 → 23]   [14 → ?]

P 35   Q 19   R 31   S 17   T 39

Analogy 11

[16 → 32]   [2 → 4]   [4 → ?]

A 12   B 11   C 8   D 2   E 3

Analogy 12

[114 → 112]   [54 → 51]   [42 → ?]

P 44   Q 38   R 46   S 6   T 4

Analogy 13

[66 → 68]   [18 → 21]   [180 → ?]

A 6   B 193   C 4   D 184   E 194

Analogy 14

[210 → 204]   [72 → 66]   [30 → ?]

P 24   Q 27   R 6   S 23   T 7

Analogy 15

[3 → 6]   [6 → 15]   [8 → ?]

A 11   B 26   C 12   D 30   E 21

Analogy 16

[6 → 12]   [8 → 16]   [14 → ?]

P 12   Q 16   R 34   S 31   T 28

Analogy 17

[276 → 270]   [186 → 180]   [90 → ?]

A 89   B 6   C 84   D 7   E 92

Analogy 18

[18 → 37]   [12 → 25]   [14 → ?]

P 16   Q 35   R 33   S 13   T 29

Analogy 19

[4 → 9]   [20 → 41]   [12 → ?]

A 14   B 12   C 28   D 25   E 34

Analogy 20

[192 → 188]   [294 → 290]   [222 → ?]

P 218   Q 6   R 227   S 5   T 222

Analogy 21

[210 → 211]   [264 → 265]   [30 → ?]

[A] 37   [B] 1   [C] 31   [D] 2   [E] 32

Analogy 22

[834 → 8340]   [546 → 5460]   [366 → ?]

[P] 3659   [Q] 3296   [R] 3294   [S] 3664   [T] 3660

Analogy 23

[84 → 840]   [744 → 7440]   [12 → ?]

[A] 110   [B] 119   [C] 120   [D] 125   [E] 109

Analogy 24

[288 → 280]   [36 → 28]   [156 → ?]

[P] 148   [Q] 154   [R] 147   [S] 8   [T] 6

Analogy 25

[108 → 109]   [60 → 62]   [126 → ?]

A 5   B 1   C 133   D 129   E 137

Analogy 26

[84 → 78]   [294 → 288]   [282 → ?]

P 5   Q 275   R 276   S 281   T 8

Analogy 27

[3 → 7]   [4 → 10]   [6 → ?]

A 9   B 23   C 18   D 16   E 8

Analogy 28

[288 → 286]   [102 → 100]   [138 → ?]

P 139   Q 4   R 142   S 1   T 136

Analogy 29

[16 → 176]   [2 → 22]   [18 → ?]

A 205   B 178   C 198   D 180   E 202

Analogy 30

[6 → 66]   [10 → 110]   [12 → ?]

P 120   Q 122   R 131   S 132   T 133

Analogy 31

[420 → 4200]   [468 → 4680]   [396 → ?]

A 3969   B 3965   C 3562   D 3960   E 3566

Analogy 32

[138 → 1380]   [186 → 1860]   [12 → ?]

P 110   Q 127   R 108   S 120   T 125

12

Analogy 33

[16 → 176]   [18 → 198]   [8 → ?]

A 87   B 81   C 98   D 88   E 80

Analogy 34

[228 → 224]   [120 → 116]   [252 → ?]

P 248   Q 2   R 5   S 247   T 249

Analogy 35

[16 → 33]   [6 → 13]   [12 → ?]

A 28   B 14   C 25   D 35   E 13

Analogy 36

[198 → 184]   [264 → 250]   [60 → ?]

P 56   Q 16   R 12   S 46   T 45

Analogy 37

[1 → 3]   [6 → 18]   [12 → ?]

A 26   B 36   C 25   D 43   E 40

Analogy 38

[96 → 92]   [288 → 284]   [198 → ?]

P 197   Q 195   R 194   S 2   T 6

Analogy 39

[18 → 35]   [6 → 11]   [12 → ?]

A 23   B 13   C 28   D 33   E 10

Analogy 40

[114 → 102]   [198 → 186]   [150 → ?]

P 138   Q 140   R 13   S 144   T 10

Analogy 41

[102 → 98]   [138 → 133]   [42 → ?]

A 5   B 36   C 46   D 7   E 38

Analogy 42

[1 → 3]   [6 → 18]   [8 → ?]

P 29   Q 18   R 24   S 28   T 17

Analogy 43

[66 → 52]   [180 → 166]   [174 → ?]

A 169   B 12   C 166   D 160   E 13

Analogy 44

[150 → 136]   [54 → 40]   [168 → ?]

P 154   Q 16   R 160   S 15   T 162

15

Analogy 45

[2 → 6]   [6 → 18]   [10 → ?]

A 36   B 29   C 19   D 18   E 30

Analogy 46

[20 → 220]   [10 → 110]   [12 → ?]

P 131   Q 119   R 120   S 138   T 132

Analogy 47

[4 → 12]   [6 → 18]   [8 → ?]

A 14   B 24   C 16   D 27   E 34

Analogy 48

[16 → 33]   [4 → 9]   [6 → ?]

P 9   Q 22   R 7   S 13   T 16

16

Analogy 49

[150 → 1500]   [120 → 1200]   [90 → ?]

A 904   B 907   C 811   D 809   E 900

Analogy 50

[150 → 142]   [168 → 160]   [108 → ?]

P 8   Q 10   R 100   S 109   T 107

Analogy 51

[294 → 302]   [72 → 80]   [42 → ?]

A 57   B 8   C 49   D 50   E 9

Analogy 52

[192 → 1920]   [102 → 1020]   [792 → ?]

P 7927   Q 7928   R 7128   S 7130   T 7920

Analogy 53

[498 → 4980]   [378 → 3780]   [174 → ?]

A 1740   B 1568   C 1747   D 1750   E 1566

Analogy 54

[1 → 3]   [4 → 12]   [10 → ?]

P 22   Q 21   R 30   S 31   T 34

Analogy 55

[16 → 32]   [22 → 44]   [12 → ?]

A 11   B 31   C 24   D 30   E 13

Analogy 56

[2 → 4]   [4 → 8]   [10 → ?]

P 9   Q 20   R 12   S 26   T 23

Analogy 57

[1 → 3]   [6 → 18]   [10 → ?]

A 36   B 38   C 21   D 30   E 22

Analogy 58

[240 → 230]   [114 → 104]   [120 → ?]

P 11   Q 109   R 115   S 10   T 110

Analogy 59

[96 → 98]   [60 → 63]   [12 → ?]

A 21   B 4   C 16   D 2   E 26

Analogy 60

[5 → 18]   [7 → 24]   [9 → ?]

P 22   Q 30   R 23   S 37   T 33

Analogy 61

[18 → 36]   [8 → 16]   [24 → ?]

A 48   B 53   C 56   D 25   E 24

Analogy 62

[180 → 181]   [132 → 134]   [108 → ?]

P 3   Q 5   R 113   S 111   T 120

Analogy 63

[2 → 4]   [22 → 44]   [14 → ?]

A 38   B 13   C 34   D 28   E 14

Analogy 64

[36 → 50]   [276 → 290]   [168 → ?]

P 189   Q 12   R 186   S 14   T 182

Analogy 65

[16 → 29]   [12 → 21]   [14 → ?]

A 26   B 10   C 25   D 11   E 30

Analogy 66

[3 → 10]   [6 → 19]   [9 → ?]

P 28   Q 38   R 30   S 18   T 19

Analogy 67

[6 → 15]   [8 → 19]   [14 → ?]

A 16   B 31   C 15   D 34   E 41

Analogy 68

[192 → 186]   [162 → 156]   [156 → ?]

P 157   Q 155   R 6   S 5   T 150

Analogy 69

[3 → 11]   [5 → 17]   [9 → ?]

A 22   B 39   C 36   D 18   E 29

Analogy 70

[4 → 12]   [6 → 18]   [10 → ?]

P 35   Q 30   R 38   S 20   T 22

Analogy 71

[4 → 44]   [8 → 88]   [12 → ?]

A 136   B 120   C 140   D 118   E 132

Analogy 72

[102 → 103]   [150 → 152]   [72 → ?]

P 84   Q 4   R 3   S 74   T 75

1) Number Analogies / Quantitative Relationships

Analogy 73

[8 → 88]　　　　[10 → 110]　　　　[12 → ?]

A 120　　　B 132　　　C 119　　　D 135　　　E 141

Analogy 74

[2 → 22]　　　　[10 → 110]　　　　[12 → ?]

P 135　　　Q 121　　　R 132　　　S 140　　　T 118

Analogy 75

[96 → 100]　　　　[120 → 125]　　　　[90 → ?]

A 101　　　B 4　　　C 7　　　D 105　　　E 96

Analogy 76

[3 → 10]　　　　[7 → 22]　　　　[9 → ?]

P 33　　　Q 37　　　R 28　　　S 20　　　T 21

Analogy 77

[18 → 36]   [10 → 20]   [12 → ?]

A 12   B 24   C 27   D 11   E 23

Analogy 78

[5 → 16]   [7 → 22]   [9 → ?]

P 20   Q 38   R 18   S 28   T 29

Analogy 79

[138 → 128]   [186 → 176]   [60 → ?]

A 49   B 56   C 9   D 50   E 10

Analogy 80

[96 → 108]   [192 → 204]   [264 → ?]

P 12   Q 276   R 277   S 13   T 285

Analogy 81

[18 → 14]   [132 → 127]   [24 → ?]

A 18   **B** 25   **C** 8   **D** 6   **E** 26

Analogy 82

[54 → 50]   [120 → 115]   [78 → ?]

P 72   **Q** 5   **R** 81   **S** 76   **T** 6

Analogy 83

[5 → 18]   [6 → 21]   [7 → ?]

A 15   **B** 18   **C** 24   **D** 30   **E** 34

Analogy 84

[4 → 44]   [20 → 220]   [10 → ?]

P 110   **Q** 99   **R** 101   **S** 112   **T** 120

Analogy 85

[228 → 226]   [36 → 34]   [198 → ?]

A 201   B 0   C 2   D 200   E 196

Analogy 86

[2 → 4]   [20 → 40]   [4 → ?]

P 8   Q 16   R 4   S 10   T 5

Analogy 87

[768 → 7680]   [102 → 1020]   [246 → ?]

A 2468   B 2216   C 2460   D 2464   E 2213

Analogy 88

[2 → 22]   [8 → 88]   [12 → ?]

P 132   Q 138   R 121   S 136   T 120

Analogy 89

[16 → 32]   [4 → 8]   [10 → ?]

A 20   B 12   C 23   D 24   E 10

Analogy 90

[66 → 64]   [216 → 214]   [282 → ?]

P 1   Q 289   R 286   S 280   T 2

Analogy 91

[16 → 176]   [20 → 220]   [6 → ?]

A 68   B 59   C 66   D 61   E 70

Analogy 92

[288 → 286]   [162 → 160]   [24 → ?]

P 22   Q 0   R 25   S 31   T 1

Analogy 93

[72 → 70]   [24 → 22]   [60 → ?]

A 64   B 2   C 0   D 58   E 59

Analogy 94

[4 → 9]   [8 → 21]   [9 → ?]

P 30   Q 31   R 24   S 14   T 15

Analogy 95

[18 → 198]   [4 → 44]   [14 → ?]

A 138   B 157   C 154   D 159   E 139

Analogy 96

[114 → 116]   [162 → 165]   [120 → ?]

P 134   Q 2   R 131   S 124   T 5

Analogy 97

[564 → 5640]   [54 → 540]   [60 → ?]

A 600   B 538   C 539   D 609   E 608

Analogy 98

[198 → 199]   [24 → 26]   [12 → ?]

P 18   Q 22   R 15   S 5   T 4

Analogy 99

[24 → 48]   [8 → 16]   [10 → ?]

A 10   B 19   C 29   D 12   E 20

Analogy 100

[258 → 252]   [186 → 180]   [156 → ?]

P 150   Q 4   R 7   S 159   T 157

Analogy 101

[5 → 13]   [8 → 22]   [9 → ?]

A 15   B 25   C 17   D 29   E 33

Analogy 102

[16 → 34]   [10 → 22]   [14 → ?]

P 18   Q 32   R 16   S 31   T 30

Analogy 103

[1 → 3]   [2 → 6]   [12 → ?]

A 36   B 41   C 43   D 26   E 25

Analogy 104

[66 → 67]   [132 → 134]   [84 → ?]

P 88   Q 87   R 93   S 4   T 1

Analogy 105

[66 → 67]   [102 → 104]   [174 → ?]

A 5   B 185   C 177   D 182   E 3

Analogy 106

[2 → 6]   [8 → 24]   [10 → ?]

P 18   Q 33   R 34   S 30   T 21

Analogy 107

[18 → 198]   [2 → 22]   [14 → ?]

A 154   B 142   C 141   D 157   E 158

Analogy 108

[96 → 82]   [54 → 40]   [204 → ?]

P 16   Q 13   R 190   S 189   T 199

Analogy 109

[192 → 194]   [18 → 20]   [180 → ?]

A 181   B 2   C 0   D 182   E 187

Analogy 110

[84 → 88]   [264 → 268]   [282 → ?]

P 291   Q 288   R 3   S 286   T 5

Analogy 111

[240 → 2400]   [12 → 120]   [750 → ?]

A 6750   B 6748   C 7501   D 7499   E 7500

Analogy 112

[48 → 45]   [12 → 8]   [60 → ?]

P 4   Q 56   R 59   S 5   T 55

Analogy 113

[3 → 10]　　　[4 → 13]　　　[9 → ?]

A 31　　　B 17　　　C 33　　　D 28　　　E 19

Analogy 114

[18 → 28]　　　[102 → 112]　　　[126 → ?]

P 9　　　Q 140　　　R 10　　　S 136　　　T 145

Analogy 115

[180 → 177]　　　[24 → 20]　　　[174 → ?]

A 178　　　B 169　　　C 3　　　D 170　　　E 5

Analogy 116

[498 → 4980]　　　[708 → 7080]　　　[504 → ?]

P 4536　　　Q 4534　　　R 5046　　　S 5045　　　T 5040

Analogy 117

[6 → 18]   [8 → 24]   [10 → ?]

A 18   B 30   C 39   D 20   E 29

Analogy 118

[144 → 132]   [72 → 60]   [252 → ?]

P 12   Q 242   R 13   S 241   T 240

Analogy 119

[22 → 44]   [24 → 48]   [12 → ?]

A 24   B 10   C 27   D 33   E 13

Analogy 120

[4 → 10]   [5 → 13]   [7 → ?]

P 19   Q 10   R 21   S 20   T 12

Analogy 1	A	B	C	**D**	E	(D) 4740	Multiply by 10.
Analogy 2	P	Q	R	S	**T**	(T) 129	Add 1. Then add 2. Then add 3
Analogy 3	A	B	C	D	**E**	(E) 36	Multiply by 3.
Analogy 4	P	Q	R	**S**	T	(S) 29	Multiply by 2. Add 1
Analogy 5	A	B	C	D	**E**	(E) 12	Multiply by 2.
Analogy 6	P	Q	R	**S**	T	(S) 133	Minus 3. Then minus 4. Then minus 5
Analogy 7	A	B	C	**D**	E	(D) 30	Multiply by 3.
Analogy 8	P	**Q**	R	S	T	(Q) 30	Multiply by 2. Add 2
Analogy 9	A	B	C	**D**	E	(D) 29	Multiply by 2. Add 1
Analogy 10	P	Q	**R**	S	T	(R) 31	Multiply by 2. Add 3

Analogy 11	A	B	**C**	D	E	(C) 8	Multiply by 2.
Analogy 12	P	**Q**	R	S	T	(Q) 38	Minus 2. Then minus 3. Then minus 4
Analogy 13	A	B	C	**D**	E	(D) 184	Add 2. Then add 3. Then add 4
Analogy 14	**P**	Q	R	S	T	(P) 24	Minus 6
Analogy 15	A	B	C	D	**E**	(E) 21	Multiply by 3. Minus 3
Analogy 16	P	Q	R	S	**T**	(T) 28	Multiply by 2.
Analogy 17	A	B	**C**	D	E	(C) 84	Minus 6
Analogy 18	P	Q	R	S	**T**	(T) 29	Multiply by 2. Add 1
Analogy 19	A	B	C	**D**	E	(D) 25	Multiply by 2. Add 1
Analogy 20	**P**	Q	R	S	T	(P) 218	Minus 4

Analogy 21	A	B	**C**	D	E	(C) 31	Add 1
Analogy 22	P	Q	R	S	**T**	(T) 3660	Multiply by 10.
Analogy 23	A	B	**C**	D	E	(C) 120	Multiply by 10.
Analogy 24	**P**	Q	R	S	T	(P) 148	Minus 8
Analogy 25	A	B	C	**D**	E	(D) 129	Add 1. Then add 2. Then add 3
Analogy 26	P	Q	**R**	S	T	(R) 276	Minus 6
Analogy 27	A	B	C	**D**	E	(D) 16	Multiply by 3. Minus 2
Analogy 28	P	Q	R	S	**T**	(T) 136	Minus 2
Analogy 29	A	B	**C**	D	E	(C) 198	Multiply by 11.
Analogy 30	P	Q	R	**S**	T	(S) 132	Multiply by 11.

Analogy 31	A	B	C	**D**	E	(D) 3960	Multiply by 10.
Analogy 32	P	Q	R	**S**	T	(S) 120	Multiply by 10.
Analogy 33	A	B	C	**D**	E	(D) 88	Multiply by 11.
Analogy 34	**P**	Q	R	S	T	(P) 248	Minus 4
Analogy 35	A	B	**C**	D	E	(C) 25	Multiply by 2. Add 1
Analogy 36	P	Q	R	**S**	T	(S) 46	Minus 14
Analogy 37	A	**B**	C	D	E	(B) 36	Multiply by 3.
Analogy 38	P	Q	**R**	S	T	(R) 194	Minus 4
Analogy 39	**A**	B	C	D	E	(A) 23	Multiply by 2. Minus 1
Analogy 40	**P**	Q	R	S	T	(P) 138	Minus 12

Analogy 41	A	**B**	C	D	E	(B) 36	Minus 4. Then minus 5. Then minus 6
Analogy 42	P	Q	**R**	S	T	(R) 24	Multiply by 3.
Analogy 43	A	B	C	**D**	E	(D) 160	Minus 14
Analogy 44	**P**	Q	R	S	T	(P) 154	Minus 14
Analogy 45	A	B	C	D	**E**	(E) 30	Multiply by 3.
Analogy 46	P	Q	R	S	**T**	(T) 132	Multiply by 11.
Analogy 47	A	**B**	C	D	E	(B) 24	Multiply by 3.
Analogy 48	P	Q	R	**S**	T	(S) 13	Multiply by 2. Add 1
Analogy 49	A	B	C	D	**E**	(E) 900	Multiply by 10.
Analogy 50	P	Q	**R**	S	T	(R) 100	Minus 8

Analogy 51	A	B	C	**D**	E	(D) 50	Add 8
Analogy 52	P	Q	R	S	**T**	(T) 7920	Multiply by 10.
Analogy 53	**A**	B	C	D	E	(A) 1740	Multiply by 10.
Analogy 54	P	Q	**R**	S	T	(R) 30	Multiply by 3.
Analogy 55	A	B	**C**	D	E	(C) 24	Multiply by 2.
Analogy 56	P	**Q**	R	S	T	(Q) 20	Multiply by 2.
Analogy 57	A	B	C	**D**	E	(D) 30	Multiply by 3.
Analogy 58	P	Q	R	S	**T**	(T) 110	Minus 10
Analogy 59	A	B	**C**	D	E	(C) 16	Add 2. Then add 3. Then add 4
Analogy 60	P	**Q**	R	S	T	(Q) 30	Multiply by 3. Add 3

Analogy 61	**A**	B	C	D	E	(A) 48	Multiply by 2.
Analogy 62	P	Q	R	**S**	T	(S) 111	Add 1. Then add 2. Then add 3
Analogy 63	A	B	C	**D**	E	(D) 28	Multiply by 2.
Analogy 64	P	Q	R	S	**T**	(T) 182	Add 14
Analogy 65	A	B	**C**	D	E	(C) 25	Multiply by 2. Minus 3
Analogy 66	**P**	Q	R	S	T	(P) 28	Multiply by 3. Add 1
Analogy 67	A	**B**	C	D	E	(B) 31	Multiply by 2. Add 3
Analogy 68	P	Q	R	S	**T**	(T) 150	Minus 6
Analogy 69	A	B	C	D	**E**	(E) 29	Multiply by 3. Add 2
Analogy 70	P	**Q**	R	S	T	(Q) 30	Multiply by 3.

Analogy 71	A	B	C	D	**E**	(E) 132	Multiply by 11.
Analogy 72	P	Q	R	S	**T**	(T) 75	Add 1. Then add 2. Then add 3
Analogy 73	A	**B**	C	D	E	(B) 132	Multiply by 11.
Analogy 74	P	Q	**R**	S	T	(R) 132	Multiply by 11.
Analogy 75	A	B	C	D	**E**	(E) 96	Add 4. Then add 5. Then add 6
Analogy 76	P	Q	**R**	S	T	(R) 28	Multiply by 3. Add 1
Analogy 77	A	**B**	C	D	E	(B) 24	Multiply by 2.
Analogy 78	P	Q	R	**S**	T	(S) 28	Multiply by 3. Add 1
Analogy 79	A	B	C	**D**	E	(D) 50	Minus 10
Analogy 80	P	**Q**	R	S	T	(Q) 276	Add 12

Analogy 81	**A**	B	C	D	E	(A) 18	Minus 4. Then minus 5. Then minus 6
Analogy 82	**P**	Q	R	S	T	(P) 72	Minus 4. Then minus 5. Then minus 6
Analogy 83	A	B	**C**	D	E	(C) 24	Multiply by 3. Add 3
Analogy 84	**P**	Q	R	S	T	(P) 110	Multiply by 11.
Analogy 85	A	B	C	D	**E**	(E) 196	Minus 2
Analogy 86	**P**	Q	R	S	T	(P) 8	Multiply by 2.
Analogy 87	A	B	**C**	D	E	(C) 2460	Multiply by 10.
Analogy 88	**P**	Q	R	S	T	(P) 132	Multiply by 11.
Analogy 89	**A**	B	C	D	E	(A) 20	Multiply by 2.
Analogy 90	P	Q	R	**S**	T	(S) 280	Minus 2

Analogy 91	A	B	C	D	E	(C) 66	Multiply by 11.
Analogy 92	P	Q	R	S	T	(P) 22	Minus 2
Analogy 93	A	B	C	D	E	(D) 58	Minus 2
Analogy 94	P	Q	R	S	T	(R) 24	Multiply by 3. Minus 3
Analogy 95	A	B	C	D	E	(C) 154	Multiply by 11.
Analogy 96	P	Q	R	S	T	(S) 124	Add 2. Then add 3. Then add 4
Analogy 97	A	B	C	D	E	(A) 600	Multiply by 10.
Analogy 98	P	Q	R	S	T	(R) 15	Add 1. Then add 2. Then add 3
Analogy 99	A	B	C	D	E	(E) 20	Multiply by 2.
Analogy 100	P	Q	R	S	T	(P) 150	Minus 6

Analogy 101	A	**B**	C	D	E	(B) 25	Multiply by 3. Minus 2
Analogy 102	P	Q	R	S	**T**	(T) 30	Multiply by 2. Add 2
Analogy 103	**A**	B	C	D	E	(A) 36	Multiply by 3.
Analogy 104	P	**Q**	R	S	T	(Q) 87	Add 1. Then add 2. Then add 3
Analogy 105	A	B	**C**	D	E	(C) 177	Add 1. Then add 2. Then add 3
Analogy 106	P	Q	R	**S**	T	(S) 30	Multiply by 3.
Analogy 107	**A**	B	C	D	E	(A) 154	Multiply by 11.
Analogy 108	P	Q	**R**	S	T	(R) 190	Minus 14
Analogy 109	A	B	C	**D**	E	(D) 182	Add 2
Analogy 110	P	Q	R	**S**	T	(S) 286	Add 4

1) Number Analogies / Quantitative Relationships Answer Sheet

Analogy 111	A	B	C	D	**E**	(E) 7500	Multiply by 10.
Analogy 112	P	Q	R	S	**T**	(T) 55	Minus 3. Then minus 4. Then minus 5
Analogy 113	A	B	C	**D**	E	(D) 28	Multiply by 3. Add 1
Analogy 114	P	Q	R	**S**	T	(S) 136	Add 10
Analogy 115	A	**B**	C	D	E	(B) 169	Minus 3. Then minus 4. Then minus 5
Analogy 116	P	Q	R	S	**T**	(T) 5040	Multiply by 10.
Analogy 117	A	**B**	C	D	E	(B) 30	Multiply by 3.
Analogy 118	P	Q	R	S	**T**	(T) 240	Minus 12
Analogy 119	**A**	B	C	D	E	(A) 24	Multiply by 2.
Analogy 120	**P**	Q	R	S	T	(P) 19	Multiply by 3. Minus 2

46

2) Number Puzzles / Equation Building

120 Puzzle Practice Questions

Grade:	3rd and 4th Grade
Level:	Level 9 and 10
Form:	7
Battery:	Quantitative Battery
Section:	2) Number Puzzles / Equation Building

2) Number Puzzles / Equation Building : 120 Questions

Puzzle 1

$$2 + 18 - 8 = 0 + ?$$

[A] 9   [B] 26   [C] 12   [D] 28   [E] 13

Puzzle 2

$$4 + 16 = 18 + ?$$

[P] 2   [Q] 18   [R] 24   [S] 9   [T] 31

Puzzle 3

$$22 - 8 = ? - 6$$

[A] 20   [B] 5   [C] 22   [D] 7   [E] 25

Puzzle 4

$$☻ + 10 = ? + 2$$
$$☻ = 4$$

[P] 2   [Q] 3   [R] 24   [S] 27   [T] 12

Puzzle 5

$? = 12 + 18$

A 35   **B** 54   **C** 42   **D** 43   **E** 30

Puzzle 6

$14 + \text{🍄} = ? - 2$

$\text{🍄} = 6$

P 32   **Q** 2   **R** 35   **S** 22   **T** 24

Puzzle 7

$20 + ? = 0 + \text{🚩}$

$\text{🚩} = 22$

A 1   **B** 2   **C** 25   **D** 15   **E** 31

Puzzle 8

$8 + 6 = ? + 14 - 10$

P 33   **Q** 10   **R** 26   **S** 11   **T** 31

Puzzle 9

$? - 10 = 14 + 4$

A 3   **B** 26   **C** 10   **D** 28   **E** 47

Puzzle 10

$1 + 15 + 8 > ?$

P 33   **Q** 34   **R** 6   **S** 42   **T** 31

Puzzle 11

$? < 14 + 14 + 14$

A 16   **B** 66   **C** 75   **D** 44   **E** 79

Puzzle 12

$12 + 4 < ?$

P 1   **Q** 4   **R** 5   **S** 23   **T** 9

51

Puzzle 13

$$18 - \,? \; = \; \mathbb{C} - 29$$
$$\mathbb{C} \; = \; 30$$

A 16   B 17   C 1   D 25   E 29

Puzzle 14

$$? + 8 \; = \; 28 - 18$$

P 0   Q 2   R 7   S 25   T 13

Puzzle 15

$$2 \; = \; ? - 20$$

A 22   B 23   C 7   D 10   E 29

Puzzle 16

$$\bigcap + 8 \; = \; ? - 2$$
$$\bigcap \; = \; 18$$

P 39   Q 9   R 25   S 43   T 28

Puzzle 17

$$16 = ? + 8$$

[A] 2   [B] 35   [C] 36   [D] 8   [E] 9

Puzzle 18

$$0 + ? < 17$$

[P] 32   [Q] 33   [R] 25   [S] 10   [T] 31

Puzzle 19

$$8 - 9 + 2 = 16 - ?$$

[A] 19   [B] 22   [C] 7   [D] 44   [E] 15

Puzzle 20

$$16 + 6 + 1 > ?$$

[P] 34   [Q] 37   [R] 23   [S] 10   [T] 27

Puzzle 21

$? + 2 \; < \; 14$

A) 18   B) 19   C) 4   D) 23   E) 12

Puzzle 22

$8 - 6 \; = \; 2 - 4 + ?$

P) 33   Q) 4   R) 7   S) 29   T) 31

Puzzle 23

$3 + 1 + 4 \; = \; 4 + ?$

A) 32   B) 4   C) 25   D) 28   E) 30

Puzzle 24

$10 + 8 \; = \; ?$

P) 16   Q) 18   R) 3   S) 36   T) 25

Puzzle 25

$$3 + 10 + 14 \quad > \quad ?$$

[A] 34   [B] 50   [C] 37   [D] 14   [E] 30

Puzzle 26

$$? + 2 + 8 \quad < \quad 15 + 12$$

[P] 17   [Q] 34   [R] 6   [S] 28   [T] 29

Puzzle 27

$$12 + 10 \quad > \quad 12 - ? + 10$$

[A] 18   [B] 22   [C] 8   [D] 25   [E] 29

Puzzle 28

$$12 + 4 \quad = \quad ? + 4 + 4$$

[P] 32   [Q] 33   [R] 20   [S] 8   [T] 24

Puzzle 29

$$? - 9 = 18 + 14 - 31$$

A 0   **B** 17   **C** 2   **D** 10   **E** 28

Puzzle 30

$$8 - 8 + ? = 2 + 2$$

P 18   **Q** 4   **R** 5   **S** 7   **T** 24

Puzzle 31

$$1 + ? = 6 - 18 + 16$$

A 32   **B** 3   **C** 6   **D** 23   **E** 13

Puzzle 32

$$? < 9 + 8 + 14$$

P 51   **Q** 37   **R** 57   **S** 43   **T** 14

Puzzle 33

$$1 + 5 \ = \ ? - 12$$

[A] 18   [B] 43   [C] 27   [D] 45   [E] 31

Puzzle 34

$$☻ + ? = 8 + 16$$
$$☻ = 18$$

[P] 1   [Q] 6   [R] 25   [S] 12   [T] 14

Puzzle 35

$$15 + 12 \ > \ 10 - ? + 6$$

[A] 33   [B] 34   [C] 37   [D] 8   [E] 42

Puzzle 36

$$? \ < \ 2 + 2 + 22$$

[P] 16   [Q] 35   [R] 39   [S] 26   [T] 44

Puzzle 37

$$30 - 24 = ? + 4$$

A) 2   B) 3   C) 23   D) 9   E) 27

Puzzle 38

$$1 + 8 + ? < 25 + 8$$

P) 24   Q) 9   R) 42   S) 27   T) 43

Puzzle 39

$$36 > ? + 2$$

A) 65   B) 52   C) 54   D) 41   E) 14

Puzzle 40

$$? + 6 < 17$$

P) 17   Q) 2   R) 18   S) 12   T) 13

Puzzle 41

$$3 + 1 = ? + 1 + 1$$

A 2   B 21   C 5   D 11   E 14

Puzzle 42

$$12 + 14 = \spadesuit + ?$$

$$\spadesuit = 6$$

P 19   Q 20   R 22   S 40   T 12

Puzzle 43

$$16 + 8 - 18 = 4 + ?$$

A 2   B 8   C 26   D 11   E 12

Puzzle 44

$$20 > 2 + ?$$

P 32   Q 25   R 10   S 30   T 31

Puzzle 45

$$? \quad > \quad 12 + 4$$

$\boxed{A}$ 0 $\qquad$ $\boxed{B}$ 3 $\qquad$ $\boxed{C}$ 26 $\qquad$ $\boxed{D}$ 14 $\qquad$ $\boxed{E}$ 15

Puzzle 46

$$16 - ? \quad = \quad \text{☼} - 2$$
$$\text{☼} \quad = \quad 10$$

$\boxed{P}$ 17 $\qquad$ $\boxed{Q}$ 1 $\qquad$ $\boxed{R}$ 2 $\qquad$ $\boxed{S}$ 8 $\qquad$ $\boxed{T}$ 30

Puzzle 47

$$12 + 8 + 8 \quad > \quad ?$$

$\boxed{A}$ 48 $\qquad$ $\boxed{B}$ 33 $\qquad$ $\boxed{C}$ 10 $\qquad$ $\boxed{D}$ 42 $\qquad$ $\boxed{E}$ 43

Puzzle 48

$$28 - 12 \quad = \quad ? + \text{☢}$$
$$\text{☢} \quad = \quad 6$$

$\boxed{P}$ 16 $\qquad$ $\boxed{Q}$ 19 $\qquad$ $\boxed{R}$ 38 $\qquad$ $\boxed{S}$ 22 $\qquad$ $\boxed{T}$ 10

Puzzle 49

$1 + 8 + 6 \quad > \quad ?$

A 16   B 18   C 6   D 22   E 24

Puzzle 50

$? - 8 + 6 \quad < \quad 1 + 12$

P 19   Q 21   R 23   S 8   T 25

Puzzle 51

$1 + 25 \quad = \quad ? + 4$

A 0   B 33   C 35   D 22   E 27

Puzzle 52

$? + 1 \quad < \quad 27$

P 51   Q 38   R 41   S 11   T 31

Puzzle 53

$$4 + 18 - ? = 4 - 3$$

[A] 50   [B] 19   [C] 21   [D] 5   [E] 44

Puzzle 54

$$22 - ? = 4$$

[P] 48   [Q] 33   [R] 18   [S] 25   [T] 29

Puzzle 55

$$10 + ? = 16 - 22 + 16$$

[A] 0   [B] 24   [C] 11   [D] 29   [E] 14

Puzzle 56

$$\text{☺} - ? = 10 - 8$$
$$\text{☺} = 4$$

[P] 16   [Q] 2   [R] 3   [S] 19   [T] 28

Puzzle 57

$$27 + ? = 28$$

[A] 1   [B] 17   [C] 18   [D] 22   [E] 14

Puzzle 58

$$2 + 12 > 4 - 8 + ?$$

[P] 34   [Q] 20   [R] 24   [S] 12   [T] 28

Puzzle 59

$$\text{🐧} + ? = 18 + 8$$
$$\text{🐧} = 24$$

[A] 1   [B] 2   [C] 25   [D] 11   [E] 29

Puzzle 60

$$0 + 10 = ? + 6 - 12$$

[P] 16   [Q] 20   [R] 5   [S] 22   [T] 40

Puzzle 61

$$6 = 24 - ?$$

A 1   B 18   C 36   D 39   E 40

Puzzle 62

$$? < 1 + 4 + 27$$

P 32   Q 34   R 53   S 38   T 12

Puzzle 63

$$8 - ? = \spadesuit - 20$$

$$\spadesuit = 26$$

A 32   B 2   C 22   D 7   E 28

Puzzle 64

$$23 > ? - 2$$

P 36   Q 37   R 39   S 43   T 12

Puzzle 65

$$24 = ? + 10$$

[A] 37   [B] 7   [C] 23   [D] 9   [E] 14

Puzzle 66

$$0 + ? = \text{🚩} - 2$$

$$\text{🚩} = 12$$

[P] 0   [Q] 17   [R] 36   [S] 38   [T] 10

Puzzle 67

$$24 - 18 = ?$$

[A] 33   [B] 6   [C] 10   [D] 29   [E] 15

Puzzle 68

$$6 + 19 > ? + 10 + 1$$

[P] 16   [Q] 1   [R] 22   [S] 23   [T] 26

Puzzle 69

$$28 - \, ? \quad = \quad ♘ \ + 4$$

$$♘ \quad = \quad 8$$

A 16   B 3   C 36   D 24   E 9

Puzzle 70

$$? \quad > \quad 1 + 13$$

P 9   Q 10   R 28   S 12   T 14

Puzzle 71

$$? \quad = \quad 8 + 2$$

A 1   B 21   C 23   D 25   E 10

Puzzle 72

$$? \, + \, ♞ \quad = \quad 18 + 10$$

$$♞ \quad = \quad 2$$

P 18   Q 4   R 26   S 10   T 28

66

Puzzle 73

$$5 + ? \ < \ 20$$

A) 1   B) 17   C) 18   D) 25   E) 27

Puzzle 74

$$? + 2 + 12 \ = \ 8 + 8$$

P) 2   Q) 4   R) 7   S) 10   T) 13

Puzzle 75

$$18 + ? - 18 \ = \ 16 - 2$$

A) 35   B) 3   C) 5   D) 9   E) 14

Puzzle 76

$$2 + 22 \ > \ 6 + ? - 2$$

P) 33   Q) 37   R) 21   S) 6   T) 28

Puzzle 77

$? - 18 = \Diamond - 8$

$\Diamond = 14$

A 21   B 24   C 44   D 30   E 14

Puzzle 78

$1 = 30 - ?$

P 49   Q 51   R 55   S 29   T 13

Puzzle 79

$1 + 9 = 22 - ?$

A 4   B 37   C 7   D 26   E 12

Puzzle 80

$30 - 4 = 2 + ?$

P 0   Q 16   R 20   S 39   T 24

Puzzle 81

$$8 + ? = 24$$

A 16   B 1   C 2   D 36   E 41

Puzzle 82

$$? + 1 = 16$$

P 0   Q 33   R 20   S 6   T 15

Puzzle 83

$$1 + 3 + 12 = 2 + ?$$

A 33   B 37   C 42   D 29   E 14

Puzzle 84

$$\clubsuit - 12 = 10 - ?$$
$$\clubsuit = 20$$

P 2   Q 25   R 11   S 28   T 13

Puzzle 85

16 = 12 + ?

A 17 **B** 1 **C** 4 **D** 28 **E** 29

Puzzle 86

30 - 10 = ?

P 20 **Q** 24 **R** 41 **S** 28 **T** 13

Puzzle 87

? < 16 + 4 + 4

A 6 **B** 40 **C** 26 **D** 27 **E** 47

Puzzle 88

8 - 2 = 18 - ? + 14

P 0 **Q** 52 **R** 37 **S** 55 **T** 26

Puzzle 89

$$0 + 14 \; = \; ? \; + 8 + 2$$

A 33   B 4   C 5   D 23   E 25

Puzzle 90

$$\square + 10 \; = \; 28 - ?$$
$$\square \; = \; 14$$

P 4   Q 21   R 22   S 24   T 28

Puzzle 91

$$6 + 8 - ? \; < \; 12 + 9$$

A 8   B 24   C 27   D 30   E 46

Puzzle 92

$$12 - ? + 14 \; < \; 16 + 12$$

P 16   Q 66   R 54   S 63   T 47

Puzzle 93

$$24 - ? = 14 - 10$$

A] 20   B] 36   C] 37   D] 13   E] 14

Puzzle 94

$$? - 5 = 16 + 2 - 17$$

P] 6   Q] 7   R] 10   S] 12   T] 30

Puzzle 95

$$14 + 4 = 2 + ? + 2$$

A] 32   B] 19   C] 38   D] 14   E] 15

Puzzle 96

$$? + ♖ = 18 + 10$$
$$♖ = 20$$

P] 16   Q] 2   R] 23   S] 8   T] 12

72

Puzzle 97

24 - 6 = ? - ☺

☺ = 2

A 16   B 20   C 21   D 9   E 44

Puzzle 98

? + ♟ = 28 - 12

♟ = 4

P 8   Q 42   R 12   S 28   T 29

Puzzle 99

? + 2 = 18 - 12

A 18   B 4   C 21   D 22   E 10

Puzzle 100

16 + ? - 10 = 6 + 6

P 21   Q 6   R 24   S 10   T 13

Puzzle 101

? + 18 = 26

A) 0   B) 17   C) 5   D) 8   E) 13

Puzzle 102

10 - ? < 22

P) 4   Q) 37   R) 26   S) 28   T) 30

Puzzle 103

? - 2 + 14 < 31 + 8

A) 48   B) 33   C) 2   D) 42   E) 46

Puzzle 104

0 + 8 = ☆ - ?

☆ = 28

P) 48   Q) 17   R) 20   S) 5   T) 40

Puzzle 105

$$? - \text{⚑} = 26 - 22$$

$$\text{⚑} = 20$$

A 36   B 39   C 24   D 42   E 30

Puzzle 106

$$4 + 23 + 2 \ > \ ?$$

P 53   Q 58   R 12   S 44   T 46

Puzzle 107

$$14 - 2 \ > \ 14 + 1 - ?$$

A 24   B 9   C 28   D 29   E 15

Puzzle 108

$$? - 4 = 14$$

P 1   Q 18   R 35   S 22   T 26

Puzzle 109

$$20 + ? = 24$$

A 1   **B** 33   **C** 4   **D** 24   **E** 11

Puzzle 110

$$16 - ? + 6 = 2 + 4$$

P 16   **Q** 35   **R** 22   **S** 7   **T** 31

Puzzle 111

$$? = 10 + 14$$

A 20   **B** 5   **C** 54   **D** 39   **E** 24

Puzzle 112

$$☠ - ? = 20 - 19$$
$$☠ = 14$$

P 2   **Q** 37   **R** 10   **S** 13   **T** 14

Puzzle 113

12 = ? - 10

A 49   B 51   C 37   D 22   E 29

Puzzle 114

24 - 14 = ?

P 32   Q 18   R 3   S 5   T 10

Puzzle 115

20 = 30 - ?

A 32   B 17   C 35   D 10   E 15

Puzzle 116

? < 26 + 4 + 1

P 16   Q 51   R 35   S 52   T 60

Puzzle 117

$$20 \ = \ 22 - \ ?$$

A 2　　　B 22　　　C 27　　　D 12　　　E 28

Puzzle 118

$$22 + 4 \ = \ ? \ + 18$$

P 3　　　Q 21　　　R 8　　　S 9　　　T 25

Puzzle 119

$$? \ + 4 \ = \ 26$$

A 52　　　B 22　　　C 11　　　D 29　　　E 15

Puzzle 120

$$? \ + 6 - 2 \ = \ 14 - 4$$

P 2　　　Q 35　　　R 20　　　S 6　　　T 29

2) Number Puzzles / Equation Building Answer Sheet

Puzzle	A/P	B/Q	C/R	D/S	E/T	Answer	Equation
Puzzle 1	A	B	**C**	D	E	(C) 12	$2 + 18 - 8 \;<\; 0 + 12$
Puzzle 2	**P**	Q	R	S	T	(P) 2	$18 + 2 \;>\; 4 + 16$
Puzzle 3	**A**	B	C	D	E	(A) 20	$22 - 8 \;<\; 20 - 6$
Puzzle 4	P	Q	R	S	**T**	(T) 12	$12 + 2 \;>\; 4 + 10$
Puzzle 5	A	B	C	D	**E**	(E) 30	$12 + 18 \;>\; 30$
Puzzle 6	P	Q	R	**S**	T	(S) 22	$14 + 6 \;<\; 22 - 2$
Puzzle 7	A	**B**	C	D	E	(B) 2	$0 + 22 \;>\; 20 + 2$
Puzzle 8	P	**Q**	R	S	T	(Q) 10	$8 + 6 \;<\; 10 + 14 - 10$
Puzzle 9	A	B	C	**D**	E	(D) 28	$14 + 4 \;>\; 28 - 10$
Puzzle 10	P	Q	**R**	S	T	(R) 6	$1 + 15 + 8 \;>\; 6$

Puzzle 11	A	B	C	D	E	(A) 16	16 $<$ 14 + 14 + 14
Puzzle 12	P	Q	R	S	T	(S) 23	12 + 4 $<$ 23
Puzzle 13	A	B	C	D	E	(B) 17	18 - 17 $<$ 30 - 29
Puzzle 14	P	Q	R	S	T	(Q) 2	28 - 18 $>$ 2 + 8
Puzzle 15	A	B	C	D	E	(A) 22	22 - 20 $>$ 2
Puzzle 16	P	Q	R	S	T	(T) 28	28 - 2 $>$ 18 + 8
Puzzle 17	A	B	C	D	E	(D) 8	8 + 8 $>$ 16
Puzzle 18	P	Q	R	S	T	(S) 10	0 + 10 $<$ 17
Puzzle 19	A	B	C	D	E	(E) 15	8 - 9 + 2 $<$ 16 - 15
Puzzle 20	P	Q	R	S	T	(S) 10	16 + 6 + 1 $>$ 10

Puzzle 21	A	B	C	D	E	(C) 4	$4 + 2 \quad < \quad 14$
Puzzle 22	P	Q	R	S	T	(Q) 4	$2 - 4 + 4 \quad > \quad 8 - 6$
Puzzle 23	A	B	C	D	E	(B) 4	$4 + 4 \quad > \quad 3 + 1 + 4$
Puzzle 24	P	Q	R	S	T	(Q) 18	$18 \quad > \quad 10 + 8$
Puzzle 25	A	B	C	D	E	(D) 14	$3 + 10 + 14 \quad > \quad 14$
Puzzle 26	P	Q	R	S	T	(R) 6	$6 + 2 + 8 \quad < \quad 15 + 12$
Puzzle 27	A	B	C	D	E	(C) 8	$12 + 10 \quad > \quad 12 - 8 + 10$
Puzzle 28	P	Q	R	S	T	(S) 8	$8 + 4 + 4 \quad > \quad 12 + 4$
Puzzle 29	A	B	C	D	E	(D) 10	$18 + 14 - 31 \quad > \quad 10 - 9$
Puzzle 30	P	Q	R	S	T	(Q) 4	$2 + 2 \quad > \quad 8 - 8 + 4$

81

Puzzle 31	A	**B**	C	D	E	(B) 3	$6 - 18 + 16 \quad > \quad 1 + 3$
Puzzle 32	P	Q	R	S	**T**	(T) 14	$14 \quad < \quad 9 + 8 + 14$
Puzzle 33	**A**	B	C	D	E	(A) 18	$1 + 5 \quad < \quad 18 - 12$
Puzzle 34	P	**Q**	R	S	T	(Q) 6	$8 + 16 \quad > \quad 18 + 6$
Puzzle 35	A	B	C	**D**	E	(D) 8	$15 + 12 \quad > \quad 10 - 8 + 6$
Puzzle 36	**P**	Q	R	S	T	(P) 16	$16 \quad < \quad 2 + 2 + 22$
Puzzle 37	**A**	B	C	D	E	(A) 2	$30 - 24 \quad < \quad 2 + 4$
Puzzle 38	P	**Q**	R	S	T	(Q) 9	$1 + 8 + 9 \quad < \quad 25 + 8$
Puzzle 39	A	B	C	D	**E**	(E) 14	$36 \quad > \quad 14 + 2$
Puzzle 40	P	**Q**	R	S	T	(Q) 2	$2 + 6 \quad < \quad 17$

Puzzle 41	A	B	C	D	E	(A) 2	$2 + 1 + 1 \; > \; 3 + 1$
Puzzle 42	P	Q	R	S	T	(Q) 20	$6 + 20 \; > \; 12 + 14$
Puzzle 43	A	B	C	D	E	(A) 2	$16 + 8 - 18 \; < \; 4 + 2$
Puzzle 44	P	Q	R	S	T	(R) 10	$20 \; > \; 2 + 10$
Puzzle 45	A	B	C	D	E	(C) 26	$26 \; > \; 12 + 4$
Puzzle 46	P	Q	R	S	T	(S) 8	$16 - 8 \; < \; 10 - 2$
Puzzle 47	A	B	C	D	E	(C) 10	$12 + 8 + 8 \; > \; 10$
Puzzle 48	P	Q	R	S	T	(T) 10	$28 - 12 \; < \; 10 + 6$
Puzzle 49	A	B	C	D	E	(C) 6	$1 + 8 + 6 \; > \; 6$
Puzzle 50	P	Q	R	S	T	(S) 8	$8 - 8 + 6 \; < \; 1 + 12$

Puzzle 51	A	B	C	**D**	E	(D) 22	22 + 4 > 1 + 25
Puzzle 52	P	Q	R	**S**	T	(S) 11	11 + 1 < 27
Puzzle 53	A	B	**C**	D	E	(C) 21	4 - 3 > 4 + 18 - 21
Puzzle 54	P	Q	**R**	S	T	(R) 18	4 > 22 - 18
Puzzle 55	**A**	B	C	D	E	(A) 0	10 + 0 < 16 - 22 + 16
Puzzle 56	P	**Q**	R	S	T	(Q) 2	4 - 2 < 10 - 8
Puzzle 57	**A**	B	C	D	E	(A) 1	27 + 1 < 28
Puzzle 58	P	Q	R	**S**	T	(S) 12	2 + 12 > 4 - 8 + 12
Puzzle 59	A	**B**	C	D	E	(B) 2	18 + 8 > 24 + 2
Puzzle 60	**P**	Q	R	S	T	(P) 16	0 + 10 < 16 + 6 - 12

Puzzle 61	A	B	C	D	E	(B) 18	24 - 18 > 6
Puzzle 62	P	Q	R	S	T	(T) 12	12 < 1 + 4 + 27
Puzzle 63	A	B	C	D	E	(B) 2	8 - 2 < 26 - 20
Puzzle 64	P	Q	R	S	T	(T) 12	23 > 12 - 2
Puzzle 65	A	B	C	D	E	(E) 14	24 < 14 + 10
Puzzle 66	P	Q	R	S	T	(T) 10	0 + 10 < 12 - 2
Puzzle 67	A	B	C	D	E	(B) 6	6 > 24 - 18
Puzzle 68	P	Q	R	S	T	(Q) 1	6 + 19 > 1 + 10 + 1
Puzzle 69	A	B	C	D	E	(A) 16	28 - 16 < 8 + 4
Puzzle 70	P	Q	R	S	T	(R) 28	28 > 1 + 13

Puzzle 71	A	B	C	D	E	(E) 10	$8 + 2 \; > \; 10$
Puzzle 72	P	Q	R	S	T	(R) 26	$18 + 10 \; > \; 26 + 2$
Puzzle 73	A	B	C	D	E	(A) 1	$5 + 1 \; < \; 20$
Puzzle 74	P	Q	R	S	T	(P) 2	$8 + 8 \; > \; 2 + 2 + 12$
Puzzle 75	A	B	C	D	E	(E) 14	$18 + 14 - 18 \; < \; 16 - 2$
Puzzle 76	P	Q	R	S	T	(S) 6	$2 + 22 \; > \; 6 + 6 - 2$
Puzzle 77	A	B	C	D	E	(B) 24	$24 - 18 \; < \; 14 - 8$
Puzzle 78	P	Q	R	S	T	(S) 29	$30 - 29 \; > \; 1$
Puzzle 79	A	B	C	D	E	(E) 12	$1 + 9 \; < \; 22 - 12$
Puzzle 80	P	Q	R	S	T	(T) 24	$2 + 24 \; > \; 30 - 4$

Puzzle 81	A	B	C	D	E	(A) 16	$24 \quad > \quad 8 + 16$
Puzzle 82	P	Q	R	S	T	(T) 15	$16 \quad > \quad 15 + 1$
Puzzle 83	A	B	C	D	E	(E) 14	$2 + 14 \quad > \quad 1 + 3 + 12$
Puzzle 84	P	Q	R	S	T	(P) 2	$10 - 2 \quad > \quad 20 - 12$
Puzzle 85	A	B	C	D	E	(C) 4	$16 \quad < \quad 12 + 4$
Puzzle 86	P	Q	R	S	T	(P) 20	$30 - 10 \quad < \quad 20$
Puzzle 87	A	B	C	D	E	(A) 6	$6 \quad < \quad 16 + 4 + 4$
Puzzle 88	P	Q	R	S	T	(T) 26	$8 - 2 \quad < \quad 18 - 26 + 14$
Puzzle 89	A	B	C	D	E	(B) 4	$0 + 14 \quad < \quad 4 + 8 + 2$
Puzzle 90	P	Q	R	S	T	(P) 4	$28 - 4 \quad > \quad 14 + 10$

2) Number Puzzles / Equation Building Answer Sheet

Puzzle 91	**A**	B	C	D	E	(A) 8	$6 + 8 - 8 \ < \ 12 + 9$
Puzzle 92	**P**	Q	R	S	T	(P) 16	$12 - 16 + 14 \ < \ 16 + 12$
Puzzle 93	**A**	B	C	D	E	(A) 20	$14 - 10 \ > \ 24 - 20$
Puzzle 94	**P**	Q	R	S	T	(P) 6	$6 - 5 \ < \ 16 + 2 - 17$
Puzzle 95	A	B	C	**D**	E	(D) 14	$14 + 4 \ < \ 2 + 14 + 2$
Puzzle 96	P	Q	R	**S**	T	(S) 8	$18 + 10 \ > \ 8 + 20$
Puzzle 97	A	**B**	C	D	E	(B) 20	$20 - 2 \ > \ 24 - 6$
Puzzle 98	P	Q	**R**	S	T	(R) 12	$12 + 4 \ < \ 28 - 12$
Puzzle 99	A	**B**	C	D	E	(B) 4	$18 - 12 \ > \ 4 + 2$
Puzzle 100	P	**Q**	R	S	T	(Q) 6	$16 + 6 - 10 \ < \ 6 + 6$

88

Puzzle 101	A	B	C	D	E	(D) 8	$26 > 8 + 18$
Puzzle 102	P	Q	R	S	T	(P) 4	$10 - 4 < 22$
Puzzle 103	A	B	C	D	E	(C) 2	$2 - 2 + 14 < 31 + 8$
Puzzle 104	P	Q	R	S	T	(R) 20	$0 + 8 < 28 - 20$
Puzzle 105	A	B	C	D	E	(C) 24	$26 - 22 > 24 - 20$
Puzzle 106	P	Q	R	S	T	(R) 12	$4 + 23 + 2 > 12$
Puzzle 107	A	B	C	D	E	(B) 9	$14 - 2 > 14 + 1 - 9$
Puzzle 108	P	Q	R	S	T	(Q) 18	$18 - 4 < 14$
Puzzle 109	A	B	C	D	E	(C) 4	$24 > 20 + 4$
Puzzle 110	P	Q	R	S	T	(P) 16	$16 - 16 + 6 < 2 + 4$

Puzzle						Answer	Equation
Puzzle 111	A	B	C	D	**E**	(E) 24	$10 + 14 \quad > \quad 24$
Puzzle 112	P	Q	R	**S**	T	(S) 13	$14 - 13 \quad < \quad 20 - 19$
Puzzle 113	A	B	C	**D**	E	(D) 22	$22 - 10 \quad > \quad 12$
Puzzle 114	P	Q	R	S	**T**	(T) 10	$24 - 14 \quad < \quad 10$
Puzzle 115	A	B	C	**D**	E	(D) 10	$20 \quad < \quad 30 - 10$
Puzzle 116	**P**	Q	R	S	T	(P) 16	$16 \quad < \quad 26 + 4 + 1$
Puzzle 117	**A**	B	C	D	E	(A) 2	$22 - 2 \quad > \quad 20$
Puzzle 118	P	Q	**R**	S	T	(R) 8	$22 + 4 \quad < \quad 8 + 18$
Puzzle 119	A	**B**	C	D	E	(B) 22	$22 + 4 \quad < \quad 26$
Puzzle 120	P	Q	R	**S**	T	(S) 6	$14 - 4 \quad > \quad 6 + 6 - 2$

90

3) Number Series

120 Series Practice Questions

Grade:	3rd and 4th Grade
Level:	Level 9 and 10
Form:	7
Battery:	Quantitative Battery
Section:	3) Number Series

3) Number Series : 120 Questions

Series 1

12 → 20 → 28 → 36 → 44 → ?

[A] 47   [B] 52   [C] 54   [D] 48   [E] 45

Series 2

66 → 54 → 132 → 66 → 54 → ?

[P] 138   [Q] 129   [R] 135   [S] 140   [T] 132

Series 3

84 → 102 → 108 → 84 → 102 → ?

[A] 104   [B] 108   [C] 98   [D] 111   [E] 116

Series 4

1 → 138 → 1 → 138 → 1 → ?

[P] 130   [Q] 143   [R] 138   [S] 132   [T] 128

Series 5

72 → 90 → 108 → 126 → 144 → ?

[A] 160   [B] 167   [C] 162   [D] 166   [E] 171

Series 6

44 → 52 → 61 → 71 → 82 → ?

[P] 88   [Q] 93   [R] 103   [S] 99   [T] 94

Series 7

36 → 48 → 60 → 72 → 84 → ?

[A] 96   [B] 103   [C] 90   [D] 92   [E] 95

Series 8

64 → 58 → 52 → 46 → 40 → ?

[P] 32   [Q] 43   [R] 27   [S] 29   [T] 34

94

Series 9

$$36 \rightarrow 40 \rightarrow 45 \rightarrow 51 \rightarrow 58 \rightarrow ?$$

[A] 63　　[B] 67　　[C] 70　　[D] 71　　[E] 66

Series 10

$$144 \rightarrow 144 \rightarrow 144 \rightarrow 144 \rightarrow 144 \rightarrow ?$$

[P] 142　　[Q] 151　　[R] 146　　[S] 147　　[T] 144

Series 11

$$16 \rightarrow 30 \rightarrow 44 \rightarrow 58 \rightarrow 72 \rightarrow ?$$

[A] 86　　[B] 90　　[C] 77　　[D] 80　　[E] 93

Series 12

$$28 \rightarrow 30 \rightarrow 32 \rightarrow 34 \rightarrow 36 \rightarrow ?$$

[P] 33　　[Q] 38　　[R] 28　　[S] 36　　[T] 48

Series 13

48 → 30 → 48 → 30 → 48 → ?

A 29   B 23   C 36   D 39   E 30

Series 14

120 → 90 → 120 → 90 → 120 → ?

P 86   Q 90   R 84   S 100   T 95

Series 15

4 → 5 → 7 → 10 → 14 → ?

A 12   B 21   C 28   D 13   E 19

Series 16

72 → 58 → 45 → 33 → 22 → ?

P 2   Q 17   R 12   S 18   T 10

Series 17

114 → 60 → 132 → 114 → 60 → ?

[A] 132   [B] 126   [C] 127   [D] 138   [E] 136

Series 18

32 → 30 → 28 → 26 → 24 → ?

[P] 20   [Q] 23   [R] 29   [S] 22   [T] 12

Series 19

1 → 2 → 4 → 8 → 16 → ?

[A] 32   [B] 41   [C] 34   [D] 33   [E] 24

Series 20

20 → 24 → 29 → 35 → 42 → ?

[P] 60   [Q] 50   [R] 57   [S] 43   [T] 55

Series 21

78 → 6 → 78 → 6 → 78 → ?

A 6   B 1   C 2   D 16   E 3

Series 22

44 → 40 → 36 → 32 → 28 → ?

P 20   Q 24   R 19   S 26   T 31

Series 23

8 → 16 → 32 → 64 → 128 → ?

A 261   B 256   C 262   D 252   E 250

Series 24

40 → 60 → 80 → 100 → 120 → ?

P 148   Q 140   R 135   S 133   T 138

Series 25

102 → 90 → 102 → 90 → 102 → ?

A 84   **B** 85   **C** 100   **D** 94   **E** 90

Series 26

72 → 64 → 57 → 51 → 46 → ?

P 33   **Q** 50   **R** 42   **S** 52   **T** 49

Series 27

16 → 17 → 19 → 22 → 26 → ?

A 35   **B** 31   **C** 21   **D** 24   **E** 29

Series 28

120 → 138 → 6 → 120 → 138 → ?

P 14   **Q** 2   **R** 6   **S** 9   **T** 4

Series 29

6 → 78 → 6 → 78 → 6 → ?

A 78   B 74   C 70   D 88   E 75

Series 30

4 → 7 → 13 → 25 → 49 → ?

P 89   Q 97   R 96   S 100   T 106

Series 31

40 → 42 → 45 → 49 → 54 → ?

A 60   B 65   C 53   D 66   E 68

Series 32

40 → 44 → 49 → 55 → 62 → ?

P 75   Q 70   R 65   S 63   T 73

Series 33

6 → 12 → 24 → 48 → 96 → ?

A 192   B 182   C 185   D 193   E 188

Series 34

1 → 19 → 37 → 55 → 73 → ?

P 83   Q 93   R 97   S 91   T 99

Series 35

20 → 18 → 16 → 14 → 12 → ?

A 9   B 8   C 10   D 1   E 20

Series 36

114 → 60 → 114 → 60 → 114 → ?

P 58   Q 61   R 56   S 60   T 59

Series 37

68 → 60 → 52 → 44 → 36 → ?

A 26   B 28   C 29   D 22   E 20

Series 38

68 → 82 → 96 → 110 → 124 → ?

P 138   Q 148   R 139   S 144   T 128

Series 39

64 → 66 → 68 → 70 → 72 → ?

A 71   B 74   C 70   D 69   E 82

Series 40

12 → 78 → 6 → 12 → 78 → ?

P 7   Q 1   R 15   S 6   T 14

Series 41

4 → 9 → 19 → 39 → 79 → ?

A 159   B 158   C 169   D 164   E 152

Series 42

56 → 64 → 73 → 83 → 94 → ?

P 110   Q 114   R 111   S 108   T 106

Series 43

102 → 48 → 102 → 48 → 102 → ?

A 49   B 47   C 39   D 41   E 48

Series 44

52 → 42 → 33 → 25 → 18 → ?

P 6   Q 4   R 17   S 21   T 12

Series 45

12 → 84 → 72 → 12 → 84 → ?

A 75   B 71   C 73   D 72   E 67

Series 46

32 → 36 → 41 → 47 → 54 → ?

P 62   Q 69   R 60   S 70   T 61

Series 47

24 → 90 → 24 → 90 → 24 → ?

A 86   B 90   C 92   D 95   E 94

Series 48

66 → 42 → 66 → 42 → 66 → ?

P 42   Q 40   R 48   S 43   T 52

104

Series 49

28 → 34 → 41 → 49 → 58 → ?

A 58   B 64   C 70   D 59   E 68

Series 50

2 → 5 → 11 → 23 → 47 → ?

P 95   Q 101   R 96   S 86   T 92

Series 51

56 → 72 → 88 → 104 → 120 → ?

A 134   B 143   C 126   D 136   E 128

Series 52

138 → 96 → 138 → 96 → 138 → ?

P 102   Q 96   R 106   S 104   T 98

Series 53

8 → 15 → 29 → 57 → 113 → ?

A 223   B 220   C 232   D 217   E 225

Series 54

16 → 26 → 36 → 46 → 56 → ?

P 70   Q 64   R 66   S 59   T 72

Series 55

72 → 62 → 52 → 42 → 32 → ?

A 22   B 28   C 15   D 23   E 17

Series 56

32 → 34 → 37 → 41 → 46 → ?

P 61   Q 50   R 51   S 45   T 52

Series 57

10 → 20 → 40 → 80 → 160 → ?

A 325   B 317   C 320   D 319   E 311

Series 58

30 → 24 → 30 → 24 → 30 → ?

P 21   Q 30   R 17   S 24   T 33

Series 59

1 → 3 → 7 → 15 → 31 → ?

A 60   B 58   C 54   D 57   E 63

Series 60

2 → 4 → 8 → 16 → 32 → ?

P 67   Q 57   R 64   S 70   T 71

Series 61

12 → 25 → 51 → 103 → 207 → ?

A 416   B 419   C 412   D 424   E 415

Series 62

108 → 24 → 108 → 24 → 108 → ?

P 25   Q 24   R 23   S 15   T 32

Series 63

12 → 24 → 48 → 96 → 192 → ?

A 374   B 376   C 386   D 382   E 384

Series 64

72 → 60 → 49 → 39 → 30 → ?

P 22   Q 20   R 12   S 29   T 31

Series 65

20 → 28 → 37 → 47 → 58 → ?

[A] 70   [B] 66   [C] 77   [D] 62   [E] 76

Series 66

12 → 18 → 24 → 30 → 36 → ?

[P] 42   [Q] 40   [R] 43   [S] 51   [T] 48

Series 67

72 → 82 → 92 → 102 → 112 → ?

[A] 120   [B] 126   [C] 131   [D] 122   [E] 132

Series 68

6 → 13 → 27 → 55 → 111 → ?

[P] 213   [Q] 230   [R] 223   [S] 214   [T] 216

Series 69

18 → 132 → 18 → 132 → 18 → ?

A 140   B 135   C 132   D 122   E 129

Series 70

68 → 74 → 80 → 86 → 92 → ?

P 93   Q 97   R 102   S 108   T 98

Series 71

52 → 58 → 65 → 73 → 82 → ?

A 82   B 102   C 95   D 92   E 90

Series 72

2 → 3 → 5 → 9 → 17 → ?

P 24   Q 33   R 23   S 35   T 34

Series 73

24 → 90 → 48 → 24 → 90 → ?

A 49   **B** 50   **C** 56   **D** 48   **E** 46

Series 74

48 → 62 → 76 → 90 → 104 → ?

P 114   **Q** 111   **R** 127   **S** 118   **T** 119

Series 75

72 → 74 → 77 → 81 → 86 → ?

A 102   **B** 90   **C** 91   **D** 82   **E** 92

Series 76

6 → 84 → 138 → 6 → 84 → ?

P 138   **Q** 141   **R** 130   **S** 132   **T** 147

Series 77

10 → 19 → 37 → 73 → 145 → ?

[A] 287   [B] 289   [C] 299   [D] 281   [E] 291

Series 78

24 → 32 → 41 → 51 → 62 → ?

[P] 80   [Q] 76   [R] 66   [S] 74   [T] 72

Series 79

1 → 1 → 1 → 1 → 1 → ?

[A] 0   [B] 8   [C] 7   [D] 1   [E] 6

Series 80

12 → 24 → 36 → 48 → 60 → ?

[P] 62   [Q] 76   [R] 72   [S] 82   [T] 66

Series 81

8 → 26 → 44 → 62 → 80 → ?

[A] 94　　[B] 99　　[C] 98　　[D] 92　　[E] 90

Series 82

16 → 22 → 29 → 37 → 46 → ?

[P] 46　　[Q] 56　　[R] 54　　[S] 49　　[T] 57

Series 83

20 → 26 → 33 → 41 → 50 → ?

[A] 67　　[B] 62　　[C] 60　　[D] 55　　[E] 52

Series 84

32 → 33 → 34 → 35 → 36 → ?

[P] 36　　[Q] 47　　[R] 37　　[S] 44　　[T] 42

Series 85

44 → 50 → 56 → 62 → 68 → ?

A 72   B 70   C 76   D 71   E 74

Series 86

28 → 36 → 44 → 52 → 60 → ?

P 68   Q 65   R 64   S 66   T 77

Series 87

44 → 54 → 64 → 74 → 84 → ?

A 91   B 94   C 102   D 86   E 84

Series 88

36 → 44 → 53 → 63 → 74 → ?

P 87   Q 76   R 82   S 86   T 81

Series 89

12 → 13 → 15 → 18 → 22 → ?

[A] 26   [B] 19   [C] 27   [D] 30   [E] 22

Series 90

24 → 20 → 16 → 12 → 8 → ?

[P] 12   [Q] 4   [R] 7   [S] 2   [T] 3

Series 91

28 → 38 → 48 → 58 → 68 → ?

[A] 71   [B] 84   [C] 78   [D] 86   [E] 85

Series 92

24 → 30 → 36 → 42 → 48 → ?

[P] 48   [Q] 58   [R] 55   [S] 60   [T] 54

Series 93

16 → 18 → 21 → 25 → 30 → ?

A 39   B 28   C 36   D 46   E 38

Series 94

132 → 102 → 96 → 132 → 102 → ?

P 96   Q 90   R 103   S 87   T 101

Series 95

8 → 9 → 11 → 14 → 18 → ?

A 17   B 20   C 33   D 23   E 13

Series 96

28 → 24 → 20 → 16 → 12 → ?

P 8   Q 1   R 14   S 3   T 15

Series 97

$$108 \rightarrow 72 \rightarrow 108 \rightarrow 72 \rightarrow 108 \rightarrow \ ?$$

A) 82　　　B) 80　　　C) 72　　　D) 62　　　E) 76

Series 98

$$10 \rightarrow 21 \rightarrow 43 \rightarrow 87 \rightarrow 175 \rightarrow \ ?$$

P) 351　　　Q) 343　　　R) 354　　　S) 347　　　T) 345

Series 99

$$52 \rightarrow 54 \rightarrow 57 \rightarrow 61 \rightarrow 66 \rightarrow \ ?$$

A) 79　　　B) 64　　　C) 68　　　D) 67　　　E) 72

Series 100

$$138 \rightarrow 42 \rightarrow 108 \rightarrow 138 \rightarrow 42 \rightarrow \ ?$$

P) 108　　　Q) 100　　　R) 112　　　S) 102　　　T) 101

117

Series 101

52 → 53 → 54 → 55 → 56 → ?

[A] 58   [B] 49   [C] 67   [D] 53   [E] 57

Series 102

32 → 44 → 56 → 68 → 80 → ?

[P] 100   [Q] 102   [R] 92   [S] 101   [T] 93

Series 103

6 → 1 → 24 → 6 → 1 → ?

[A] 33   [B] 22   [C] 17   [D] 24   [E] 32

Series 104

36 → 34 → 32 → 30 → 28 → ?

[P] 26   [Q] 31   [R] 22   [S] 21   [T] 25

Series 105

6 → 90 → 138 → 6 → 90 → ?

[A] 140   [B] 138   [C] 131   [D] 137   [E] 147

Series 106

6 → 102 → 114 → 6 → 102 → ?

[P] 104   [Q] 116   [R] 115   [S] 105   [T] 114

Series 107

138 → 144 → 138 → 144 → 138 → ?

[A] 147   [B] 144   [C] 142   [D] 135   [E] 137

Series 108

64 → 62 → 60 → 58 → 56 → ?

[P] 60   [Q] 58   [R] 54   [S] 59   [T] 50

Series 109

40 → 46 → 53 → 61 → 70 → ?

[A] 80   [B] 82   [C] 84   [D] 85   [E] 78

Series 110

28 → 36 → 45 → 55 → 66 → ?

[P] 88   [Q] 78   [R] 80   [S] 86   [T] 72

Series 111

68 → 86 → 104 → 122 → 140 → ?

[A] 153   [B] 163   [C] 154   [D] 158   [E] 165

Series 112

108 → 108 → 90 → 108 → 108 → ?

[P] 93   [Q] 89   [R] 85   [S] 82   [T] 90

Series 113

$$102 \rightarrow 120 \rightarrow 138 \rightarrow 102 \rightarrow 120 \rightarrow \; ?$$

A 139　　B 141　　C 128　　D 138　　E 144

Series 114

$$114 \rightarrow 54 \rightarrow 12 \rightarrow 114 \rightarrow 54 \rightarrow \; ?$$

P 15　　Q 10　　R 13　　S 12　　T 19

Series 115

$$60 \rightarrow 48 \rightarrow 37 \rightarrow 27 \rightarrow 18 \rightarrow \; ?$$

A 2　　B 10　　C 12　　D 17　　E 20

Series 116

$$12 \rightarrow 23 \rightarrow 45 \rightarrow 89 \rightarrow 177 \rightarrow \; ?$$

P 348　　Q 353　　R 344　　S 345　　T 361

Series 117

68 → 54 → 41 → 29 → 18 → ?

A 1   B 0   C 4   D 8   E 5

Series 118

78 → 12 → 54 → 78 → 12 → ?

P 54   Q 58   R 59   S 55   T 64

Series 119

132 → 114 → 54 → 132 → 114 → ?

A 59   B 64   C 57   D 50   E 54

Series 120

84 → 84 → 84 → 84 → 84 → ?

P 84   Q 89   R 92   S 79   T 94

122

Series						Answer	Rule
Series 1	A	**B**	C	D	E	(B) 52	Add 8.
Series 2	P	Q	R	S	**T**	(T) 132	Repeat numbers [66, 54, 132].
Series 3	A	**B**	C	D	E	(B) 108	Repeat numbers [84, 102, 108].
Series 4	P	Q	**R**	S	T	(R) 138	Repeat numbers [1, 138].
Series 5	A	B	**C**	D	E	(C) 162	Add 18.
Series 6	P	Q	R	S	**T**	(T) 94	Add 8. Increment by 1.
Series 7	**A**	B	C	D	E	(A) 96	Add 12.
Series 8	P	Q	R	S	**T**	(T) 34	Minus 6.
Series 9	A	B	C	D	**E**	(E) 66	Add 4. Increment by 1.
Series 10	P	Q	R	S	**T**	(T) 144	Repeat numbers [144, 144].

123

Series						Answer	Rule
Series 11	**A**	B	C	D	E	(A) 86	Add 14.
Series 12	P	**Q**	R	S	T	(Q) 38	Add 2.
Series 13	A	B	C	D	**E**	(E) 30	Repeat numbers [48, 30].
Series 14	P	**Q**	R	S	T	(Q) 90	Repeat numbers [120, 90].
Series 15	A	B	C	D	**E**	(E) 19	Add 1. Increment by 1.
Series 16	P	Q	**R**	S	T	(R) 12	Minus 14. Increment by 1.
Series 17	**A**	B	C	D	E	(A) 132	Repeat numbers [114, 60, 132].
Series 18	P	Q	R	**S**	T	(S) 22	Minus 2.
Series 19	**A**	B	C	D	E	(A) 32	Multipy by 2.
Series 20	P	**Q**	R	S	T	(Q) 50	Add 4. Increment by 1.

Series 21	A	B	C	D	E	(A) 6	Repeat numbers [78, 6].
Series 22	P	Q	R	S	T	(Q) 24	Minus 4.
Series 23	A	B	C	D	E	(B) 256	Multipy by 2.
Series 24	P	Q	R	S	T	(Q) 140	Add 20.
Series 25	A	B	C	D	E	(E) 90	Repeat numbers [102, 90].
Series 26	P	Q	R	S	T	(R) 42	Minus 8. Increment by 1.
Series 27	A	B	C	D	E	(B) 31	Add 1. Increment by 1.
Series 28	P	Q	R	S	T	(R) 6	Repeat numbers [120, 138, 6].
Series 29	A	B	C	D	E	(A) 78	Repeat numbers [6, 78].
Series 30	P	Q	R	S	T	(Q) 97	Multipy by 2. Minus 1.

Series 31	**A**	B	C	D	E	(A) 60	Add 2. Increment by 1.
Series 32	P	**Q**	R	S	T	(Q) 70	Add 4. Increment by 1.
Series 33	**A**	B	C	D	E	(A) 192	Multipy by 2.
Series 34	P	Q	R	**S**	T	(S) 91	Add 18.
Series 35	A	B	**C**	D	E	(C) 10	Minus 2.
Series 36	P	Q	R	**S**	T	(S) 60	Repeat numbers [114, 60].
Series 37	A	**B**	C	D	E	(B) 28	Minus 8.
Series 38	**P**	Q	R	S	T	(P) 138	Add 14.
Series 39	A	**B**	C	D	E	(B) 74	Add 2.
Series 40	P	Q	R	**S**	T	(S) 6	Repeat numbers [12, 78, 6].

Series 41	A	B	C	D	E	(A) 159	Multipy by 2. Add 1.
Series 42	P	Q	R	S	T	(T) 106	Add 8. Increment by 1.
Series 43	A	B	C	D	E	(E) 48	Repeat numbers [102, 48].
Series 44	P	Q	R	S	T	(T) 12	Minus 10. Increment by 1.
Series 45	A	B	C	D	E	(D) 72	Repeat numbers [12, 84, 72].
Series 46	P	Q	R	S	T	(P) 62	Add 4. Increment by 1.
Series 47	A	B	C	D	E	(B) 90	Repeat numbers [24, 90].
Series 48	P	Q	R	S	T	(P) 42	Repeat numbers [66, 42].
Series 49	A	B	C	D	E	(E) 68	Add 6. Increment by 1.
Series 50	P	Q	R	S	T	(P) 95	Multipy by 2. Add 1.

127

3) Number Series Answer Sheet

Series 51	A	B	C	**D**	E	(D) 136	Add 16.
Series 52	P	**Q**	R	S	T	(Q) 96	Repeat numbers [138, 96].
Series 53	A	B	C	D	**E**	(E) 225	Multipy by 2. Minus 1.
Series 54	P	Q	**R**	S	T	(R) 66	Add 10.
Series 55	**A**	B	C	D	E	(A) 22	Minus 10.
Series 56	P	Q	R	S	**T**	(T) 52	Add 2. Increment by 1.
Series 57	A	B	**C**	D	E	(C) 320	Multipy by 2.
Series 58	P	Q	R	**S**	T	(S) 24	Repeat numbers [30, 24].
Series 59	A	B	C	D	**E**	(E) 63	Multipy by 2. Add 1.
Series 60	P	Q	**R**	S	T	(R) 64	Multipy by 2.

128

Series 61	A	B	C	D	E	(E) 415	Multipy by 2. Add 1.
Series 62	P	Q	R	S	T	(Q) 24	Repeat numbers [108, 24].
Series 63	A	B	C	D	E	(E) 384	Multipy by 2.
Series 64	P	Q	R	S	T	(P) 22	Minus 12. Increment by 1.
Series 65	A	B	C	D	E	(A) 70	Add 8. Increment by 1.
Series 66	P	Q	R	S	T	(P) 42	Add 6.
Series 67	A	B	C	D	E	(D) 122	Add 10.
Series 68	P	Q	R	S	T	(R) 223	Multipy by 2. Add 1.
Series 69	A	B	C	D	E	(C) 132	Repeat numbers [18, 132].
Series 70	P	Q	R	S	T	(T) 98	Add 6.

Series 71	A	B	C	**D**	E	(D) 92	Add 6. Increment by 1.
Series 72	P	**Q**	R	S	T	(Q) 33	Multipy by 2. Minus 1.
Series 73	A	B	C	**D**	E	(D) 48	Repeat numbers [24, 90, 48].
Series 74	P	Q	R	**S**	T	(S) 118	Add 14.
Series 75	A	B	C	D	**E**	(E) 92	Add 2. Increment by 1.
Series 76	**P**	Q	R	S	T	(P) 138	Repeat numbers [6, 84, 138].
Series 77	A	**B**	C	D	E	(B) 289	Multipy by 2. Minus 1.
Series 78	P	Q	R	**S**	T	(S) 74	Add 8. Increment by 1.
Series 79	A	B	C	**D**	E	(D) 1	Multipy by 2. Minus 1.
Series 80	P	Q	**R**	S	T	(R) 72	Add 12.

Series 81	A	B	C	D	E	(C) 98	Add 18.
Series 82	P	Q	R	S	T	(Q) 56	Add 6. Increment by 1.
Series 83	A	B	C	D	E	(C) 60	Add 6. Increment by 1.
Series 84	P	Q	R	S	T	(R) 37	Add 1.
Series 85	A	B	C	D	E	(E) 74	Add 6.
Series 86	P	Q	R	S	T	(P) 68	Add 8.
Series 87	A	B	C	D	E	(B) 94	Add 10.
Series 88	P	Q	R	S	T	(S) 86	Add 8. Increment by 1.
Series 89	A	B	C	D	E	(C) 27	Add 1. Increment by 1.
Series 90	P	Q	R	S	T	(Q) 4	Minus 4.

Series 91	A	B	C	D	E	(C) 78	Add 10.
Series 92	P	Q	R	S	T	(T) 54	Add 6.
Series 93	A	B	C	D	E	(C) 36	Add 2. Increment by 1.
Series 94	P	Q	R	S	T	(P) 96	Repeat numbers [132, 102, 96].
Series 95	A	B	C	D	E	(D) 23	Add 1. Increment by 1.
Series 96	P	Q	R	S	T	(P) 8	Minus 4.
Series 97	A	B	C	D	E	(C) 72	Repeat numbers [108, 72].
Series 98	P	Q	R	S	T	(P) 351	Multipy by 2. Add 1.
Series 99	A	B	C	D	E	(E) 72	Add 2. Increment by 1.
Series 100	P	Q	R	S	T	(P) 108	Repeat numbers [138, 42, 108].

Series 101	A	B	C	D	E	(E) 57	Add 1.
Series 102	P	Q	R	S	T	(R) 92	Add 12.
Series 103	A	B	C	D	E	(D) 24	Repeat numbers [6, 1, 24].
Series 104	P	Q	R	S	T	(P) 26	Minus 2.
Series 105	A	B	C	D	E	(B) 138	Repeat numbers [6, 90, 138].
Series 106	P	Q	R	S	T	(T) 114	Repeat numbers [6, 102, 114].
Series 107	A	B	C	D	E	(B) 144	Repeat numbers [138, 144].
Series 108	P	Q	R	S	T	(R) 54	Minus 2.
Series 109	A	B	C	D	E	(A) 80	Add 6. Increment by 1.
Series 110	P	Q	R	S	T	(Q) 78	Add 8. Increment by 1.

133

Series 111	A	B	C	**D**	E	(D) 158	Add 18.
Series 112	P	Q	R	S	**T**	(T) 90	Repeat numbers [108, 108, 90].
Series 113	A	B	C	**D**	E	(D) 138	Repeat numbers [102, 120, 138].
Series 114	P	Q	R	**S**	T	(S) 12	Repeat numbers [114, 54, 12].
Series 115	A	**B**	C	D	E	(B) 10	Minus 12. Increment by 1.
Series 116	P	**Q**	R	S	T	(Q) 353	Multipy by 2. Minus 1.
Series 117	A	B	C	**D**	E	(D) 8	Minus 14. Increment by 1.
Series 118	**P**	Q	R	S	T	(P) 54	Repeat numbers [78, 12, 54].
Series 119	A	B	C	D	**E**	(E) 54	Repeat numbers [132, 114, 54].
Series 120	**P**	Q	R	S	T	(P) 84	Repeat numbers [84, 84].

Made in the USA
San Bernardino, CA
09 November 2018